AUTISM
SPECTRUM REALITIES

Gary W. Studebaker Ed.D.

TheSpectrumPress@gmail.com

Made in the USA
Charleston, SC

ISBN: 1453739696
ISBN-13: 9781453739693
LCCN: 2010911801

ACKNOWLEDGEMENTS

Numerous persons have made contributions toward my writing "Autism Spectrum Realities." A sincere thank you goes to these individuals:

- Ramona, my daughter, added to my appreciation of autism as a parent, special education instructor and writer. She was diagnosed with autism at three years of age and continues to share the many facets of her world.

- Susan, my wife, provided the review and organization that was necessary throughout the duration of this project. Her knowledge of the autism spectrum was an invaluable resource and contribution to this work.

- Many educators, writers, researchers, psychologists and medical specialists in the field of autism have advanced my knowledge and interest in the autism spectrum.

- My writing group provided indispensible comments as they critiqued my writing for this project.

- Parent support group participants shared strategies, resources, agencies and specialists that they have found effective in this field. Support group participation is a lifelong pursuit for many parents, therefore; these individuals have become significant friends and social acquaintances.

CONTENTS

Section 1

Comments from support providers
(Educational, medical, psychological, social and technical specialists)

Section 2

Comments from parents and relatives

Section 3

Comments from persons on the autism spectrum
and innovations by Temple Grandin and Daniel Paul Tammet

PREFACE

Leo Kanner, an Austrian psychiatrist and physician gave us the first description of autism in a paper he published in 1943. In 1944, Hans Asperger, an Austrian pediatrician and child psychiatrist, published the first definition of Asperger's syndrome.

Autism spectrum disorder is a pervasive developmental disorder with mild to severe developmental challenges. This range is referred to as the spectrum. Symptoms may include disabilities in many areas including social, communication, sensory, behavior, motor and intellectual skills.

The Fourth Edition of the Diagnostic and Statistical Manual (DSM-IV) is used by medical professionals for diagnosing autism. DSM-IV categorizes the following autism and related disorders as pervasive developmental disorders (PDD):

- Autism (Autistic Disorder)

- Asperger's Syndrome

- Pervasive Developmental Disorder Not Otherwise Specified (PDDNOS)

- Rett's Disorder

- Childhood Disintegrative Disorder (CDD)

A glossary at the back of this book defines terminology associated with the autism spectrum.

This book focuses on two areas of the autism spectrum. They are autism and Asperger's syndrome.

Since the early 1990s, autism spectrum disorders have increased at an alarming rate around the world. In December of 2009, The Centers for Disease Control estimated that 1 in 110 births in the United States result in an autism spectrum diagnosis. Boys on the spectrum outnumber girls, four to one.

Presented in a poetry format, this book provides the reader with a grasp of autism spectrum realities including a wide range of challenges and coping strategies for parents, relatives, support providers and individuals on the spectrum. Persons not directly involved with autism and the associated range of concerns are educated with many thought-provoking realities.

Behavioral challenges, sensory deficits, social anxieties, medical concerns, motor problems and moral issues are explored with some strategies to deal with these areas. As people become informed, they can be part of the solution at addressing this world-wide crisis.

In 2007, the American Academy of Pediatrics recognized that pediatricians need to be better equipped to deal with the increasing number of autism spectrum disorders. Therefore, information was developed to help pediatricians recognize these disorders at the early stages of life. Pediatricians were given the responsibility to identify signs of autism, as well as developmental concerns, by questioning parents or caretakers and observing the child's behavior. They were also advised to administer a standardized autism spectrum screening on all children 18 to 24 months of age regardless of whether there were any concerns. These guidelines were implemented to prepare pediatricians to talk with parents regarding early intervention, educational strategies and therapies that need to be considered by families to address their child's difficulties.

Some individuals on the spectrum are able to live independent lives in community settings. However, the majority of persons on the spectrum remain impaired in their ability to communicate and socialize. These increasing numbers place a significant economic responsibility, as well as challenges on families, educators, medical personnel and society.

The rationale for the increase of persons with autism spectrum disorders has been widely debated with no conclusive arguments cited by the courts. However, the following theories have been proposed:

- Exposure to environmental factors including the increase of toxins and pollutants in the atmosphere, the ground and food.

- Insult to the body through the required childhood vaccines.

- More inclusive diagnostic procedures.

The federal law entitled "Individuals with Disabilities Education Act," (IDEA) of 1990 and the IDEA Amendments of 1997 were enacted by congress to update the Education for All Handicapped Children Act of 1975. Every child with a disability is guaranteed a free and appropriate education. Since then the incidence of autism in schools has risen dramatically. In 1992, the Diagnostic and Statistical Manual, refined the diagnostic criteria for an autistic disorder. Autism then became a spectrum disorder ranging from mild to a chronic disorder.

Many persons on the spectrum have informed us what their world is like and how society has enhanced as well as inhibited their progress. Some of these individuals have made major contributions as writers, inventors, artists, musicians, teachers, public speakers and entrepreneurs. The information that they have shared with us has added significantly to our knowledge as we search for ways to understand and improve the lives of these individuals.

The award-winning motion pictures "Rain Man" (1988) and "Temple Grandin" (2010) exposed the public to the lives of persons on the spectrum. The 2004 Academy Award® nominee for documentary short subject was entitled "Autism is a World." Written by Sue Rubin, the documentary increased public awareness with an intriguing account of an individual with autism. "Mozart and the Whale" (2006), presents an authentic account of a love story between two savants. This couple with Asperger's syndrome, deal with challenges to their developing relationship.

Society needs to consider many issues regarding the lives of persons on the spectrum as well as all disabled individuals. The challenges include access to an appropriate education, vocational pursuits, housing, employment, medical care, psychological and social services. Many disabled individuals continue to go through life with many of these needs inappropriately met.

The parents of children on the spectrum are experts at knowing their loved one. They are advocates and teachers for their son or daughter. They've all come to realize that their child has enormously changed their family life forever. Some parents may feel that they have made mistakes, however; these parents are often exploring new areas and the research that they needed has often not been available. Many parents have developed expertise at educating others and making contributions to research studies. Indeed, parents are the heroes in the lives of their loved ones, even though their children may not be able to communicate that feeling. Siblings also share in the caretaking responsibilities of these family members and their lives are affected accordingly.

Over the years there have been advances in training and technology received by teachers, support workers and medical personnel. Accordingly, parents have been provided with a wide selection of strategies and treatment options, many of which are costly and time consuming and must be carefully evaluated for their usefulness and feasibility for the unique needs of their child.

SECTION 1

Comments from support providers

(educational, medical, psychological, social and technical specialists)

The Unknown

Research still continues.
Our knowledge base has grown.
What's the cause of autism?
The answer is unknown.

We're looking at genetics,
Immune deficiencies,
Environmental factors,
Vaccines and allergies.

We'll no doubt solve this puzzle
With evidence conclusive.
Until that time, we've come to know
The answer is elusive.

Social Rules

Without a grasp of social rules
You're bound to get frustrated.
Yet there are many customs
That simply go unstated.

People on the spectrum
Dread these mysteries.
They make life perplexing,
These social subtleties:

How to greet a person,
Just when to empathize,
How close should I stand to him,
And why apologize,

How to say, "I'm sorry,"
Or share a conversation,
When to speak with privacy
And show appreciation.

The torment of these hidden rules
Feels like strangulation.
It then becomes prohibitive
To meet an expectation.

Unless these hidden social rules
Are analyzed and taught,
Many on the spectrum
Will go through life distraught.

A Moral Question

Without a job to give him pride
Glen lacked what he enjoyed.
Like most folks with autism
He now is unemployed.
He posed a moral question
That needs to be addressed,
"Can we ignore the jobless rate
That burdens the oppressed?"

He thought about his former years;
Employment was lean.
The times that he was working
Were few and far between.
Like everyone, he has a sense
Of pride and dignity.
Indeed, a job would set the stage
To be all that he can be.

He knew his future looked quite bleak
Based on past rejection.
"Any job would give me pride."
He said with this projection.
"If people knew what we go through
Would they still delay?
It all comes down to equal rights –
The will to find a way."

More Than Money

I teach kids on the spectrum to their specific need.
Each has an individual plan for which we've all agreed.

To give them independence has been my main concern.
I must adapt each lesson so everyone can learn.

They need daily living tasks and social skill direction.
My instructions must be clear
To make sure there's connection.

They sometimes learn through role-play
And hands-on application.
Some will need behavior plans but all need affirmation.

A natural environment is where they've often learned.
Today they're buying groceries
With money that they've earned.

My job is to motivate so each child will attend,
To make each lesson come alive so they can comprehend.

It's all about their future, I help them to prepare.
I must impart the tools they need,
To use when they get there.

It's more than just a pay check. My years have demonstrated,
It's when I go the extra mile, I'm more than compensated.

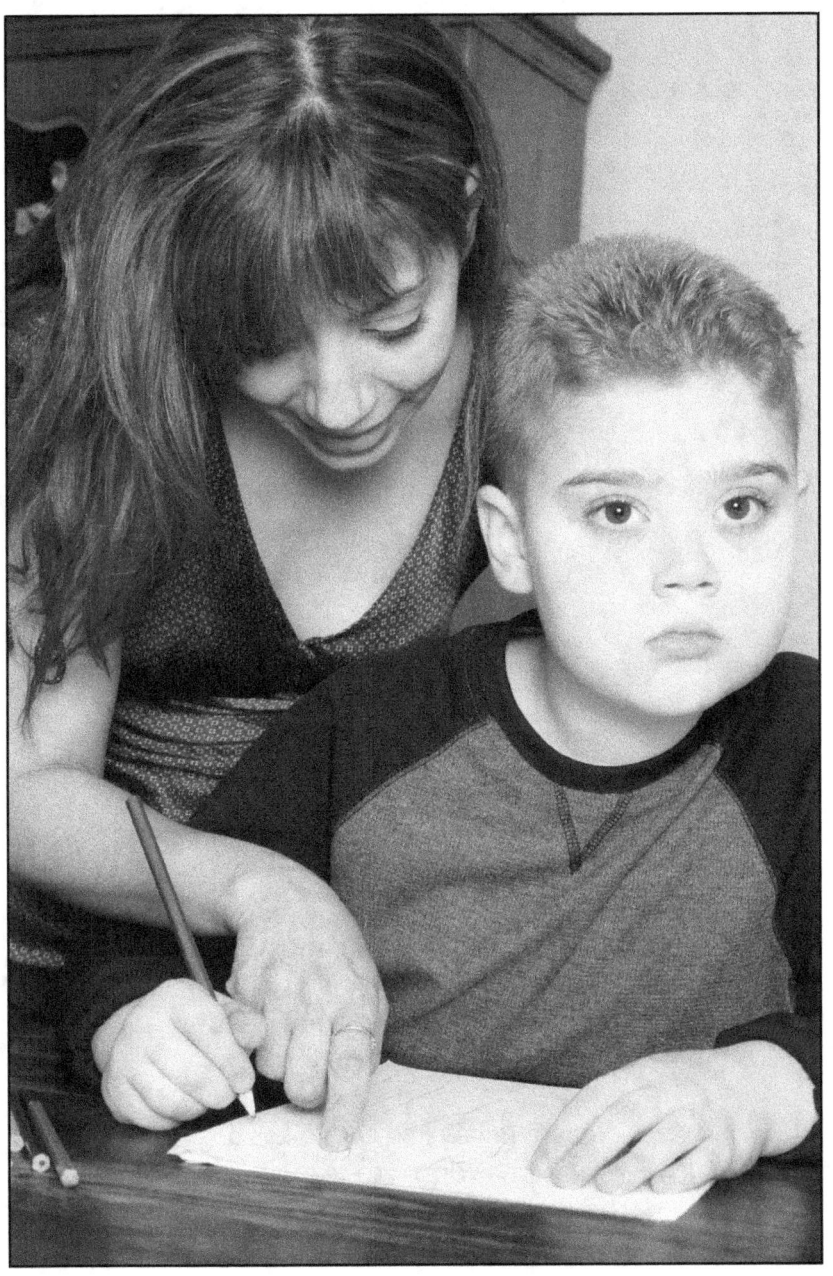

Low Places

If teachers are objective
They no doubt will confess,
Expecting low performance
Causes students to regress.

To motivate their students
There's one trait that's essential,
They must expect the students
To achieve their full potential.

Just because a student
Is in special education,
Doesn't mean the teacher
Must reduce the expectation.

If a student hasn't learned
The proper social graces,
Doesn't mean the child belongs
In unkind, lower places.

No matter the vocation,
No matter what the station,
The goal is simply meeting needs
For best participation.

Teachers have a trust to keep.
It comes down to respect.
They're called to be accountable.
That's what we all expect.

Partial Participation

Independent students
Are a teacher's chief concern.
But if teachers do their tasks for them,
How will the students learn?

Partially participate –
That's how they learn a skill.
If they can't do it all at once,
Partially they will.

The staff is trained at teaching
The whole task part by part.
They mark the student's progress
On a student profile chart.

Incentives can be useful
Whenever there's a need.
But step by step is what it takes
For students to succeed.

People First

People on the spectrum
Are seeking to connect.
But we must enter their world first
And give them our respect.

We're teaching them to travel
Through a world that's complicated.
We'll need to give them competence
Before it's navigated.

When living in a hostile land
People need protection.
Anxiety takes over
When there is no connection.

Will people follow orders
And do what we expect,
If we don't have the character
To treat them with respect?

Does learning really happen
When people are coerced?
The label may be autism,
But they are people first.

The Unexpected

Predictable environments
Help with understanding,
But if you're on the spectrum,
Change is quite demanding.

Circumstances sometimes change
From everyday tradition.
This can often bring about
Stress and opposition.

A visit with a relative,
A sudden change of schedule,
An unfamiliar setting,
Can often be quite stressful.

An eye examination,
Attendance at a wedding,
Changes from the routine
Are often quite upsetting.

By practicing ahead of time
To meet the unexpected,
Change can be less frightening
And even more accepted.

Language Instruction

For language to have meaning
It must be understood,
No matter what the dialect
Or where the neighborhood.

Many on the spectrum
Find this problematic.
Their language acquisition
Is far from automatic.

Teach them how to make it known
When they don't understand.
Non-compliance doesn't mean
They need a reprimand.

Some instructions tend to be
Perplexing and demanding.
Don't assume they comprehend.
Check for understanding.

Whatever It Takes

For many on the spectrum
It's tough to draw or write.
They need adaptations
Or a nurse to check their sight.

To keep their writing on the line,
To form the proper size,
Even writing legibly
Takes skill to visualize.

Some folks lack fine motor skills
For writing with control.
This will call for practice
To reach their writing goal.

By working on these writing skills
They learn coordination.
Some will need a pencil grip –
A writing adaptation.

Some will use a template,
Or write in gridded spaces.
A child may learn to gain control
By symbols that he traces.

For some, it may be typing.
If so then we'll pursue it.
Everyone is different so
Whatever works – we'll do it.

Yet some are highly talented
With memory and vision.
They can view a city once
Then draw it with precision.

Tangible and Teachable

There is a well-known principle
Good teachers are pursuing.
Effective learning happens
When students learn by doing.

Hands-on learning stimulates
Appeal and fascination.
Facts become more tangible
Through such participation.

Students maintain focus
And problems get resolved.
They gain the most from learning
When movement is involved.

Drawing, building, measuring,
Computer information,
Games with problem solving
Increase their motivation.

Lectures have the least appeal
As words can be deceptive.
Yet active learner's blossom
They're simply more receptive.

The Second Time Around

I use a teaching strategy
That helps my students grow.
They often get in trouble
Because they didn't know.

Instead of saying, "No" to them
I've learned a better way.
I tell them what they can do
And how they can obey.

When students learn a better way
With positive assistance,
They learn to be responsible
And comply with less resistance.

By using such a strategy
Quite often I have found,
They learn to make a better choice
The second time around.

He Got the Picture

Some people with dyslexia
Have vision that's distorted.
For some folks on the spectrum,
The same has been reported.

Words may run together,
Images are faulty.
Sometimes there are headaches
With reading difficulty.

In certain cases, colored lenses
Make the view more clear.
Scenes come into focus
And headaches disappear.

These lenses filter colors.
The visual world expands.
Exactly how this happens
No one fully understands.

Pioneered by Helen Irlen,
Colored lenses hold potential.
For some this method doesn't work
While others are successful.

Some find this method filters out
Unwanted stimuli.
For persons needing such relief
It may be worth a try.

Kurt finally saw a blade of grass
Contrasted from the dew.
At last he got the picture
When his world came into view.

Research Realities

Research shows the usefulness
Of music therapy.
For some folks on the spectrum
It's a useful strategy.

Outcomes are encouraging:
Social skills are strengthened,
Effective self-expression and
Attention skills are lengthened,

Improvement of behaviors,
Diminished agitation,
Advancement in cognition,
And less self-stimulation.

The auditory process
And motor skills advance.
Kids grow through music therapy
When given such a chance.

Expose your child to music,
That's the implication.
Parents can support their child
With such participation.

Making a Difference

Reciprocating friendship,
The selflessness of giving,
To make a contribution
Is at the heart of living.

Some seniors at a high school
Have earned a reputation;
They formed a club to mentor kids
In Special Education.

They didn't ask for payment
But voiced this point of view,
"We want to make a difference
By the very things we do."

Both parties learn that partnership
Is like a helpful brother,
Through social interaction
They learn from one another.

With social games and parties
And volunteer access,
The students that are mentored
Gain social skill success.

The volunteers are proud to know
They're part of the solution.
By teaming with their partner
They make a contribution.

Each volunteer is recognized
For teaming with a peer.
They've learned that it's empowering
To be a volunteer.

The Renowned

Kanner and Asperger
Helped unlock the mystery.
They first described autism traits,
A landmark in our history.

Back in the 1940s
Their research was explained.
How many went undiagnosed
Before that was attained?

Looking back at people's lives
Triggered speculation,
That spectrum traits were present
In a well-known population.

The list includes Da Vinci,
And Thomas Jefferson,
Mozart and Beethoven,
And Emily Dickenson,

Edison and Einstein,
Michelangelo,
Alexander Graham Bell,
Newton and Van Gogh.

Could they have had autism traits,
These legends in our history?
This issue is debated
But the answer is a mystery.

Our loved ones on the spectrum
Have gifts that must be found.
They may have related traits
Of those who are renowned.

Movement Matters

Muscles must coordinate
With signals from the brain.
For all the movements that we make
Time and time again.

We need a kinesthetic feel
Of where we are in space,
So we can move with confidence,
Harmony and grace.

Organizing input
Through movement information
Strengthens motor planning
And smooth coordination.

Motor tasks can help reduce
Over stimulation
So people on the spectrum
Can decrease a strong fixation.

Give children opportunities
For sports and recreation.
Provide some games around the house
To build coordination.

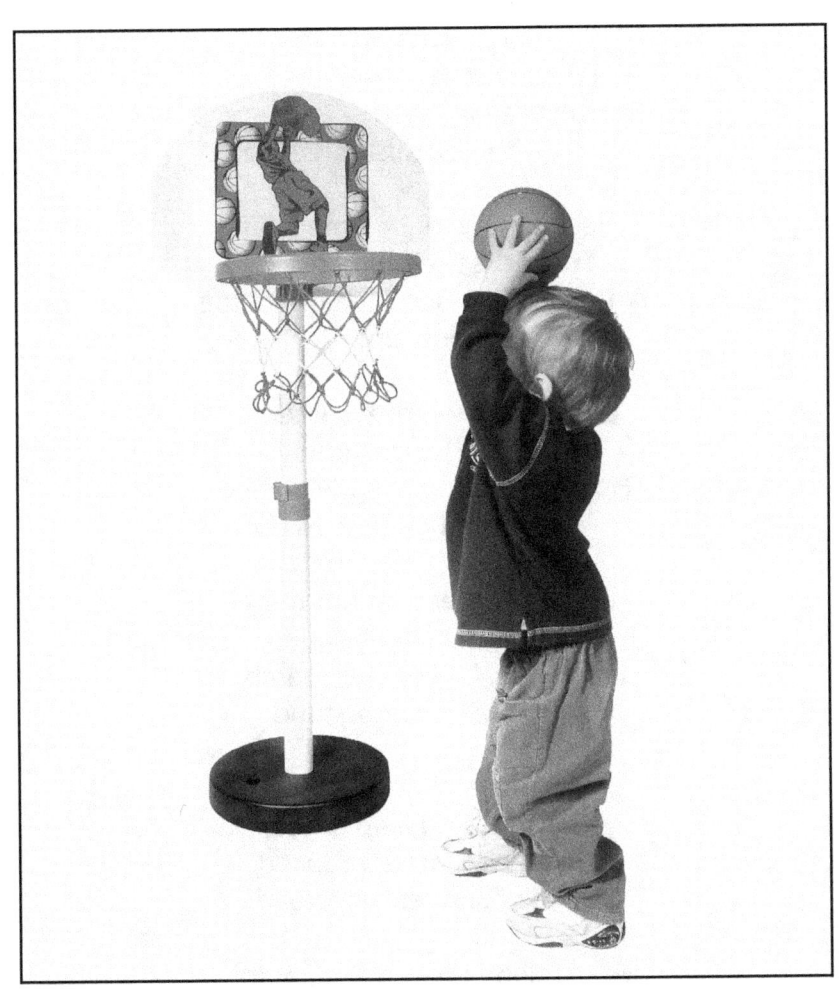

Seeing Time

Telling time is nebulous
Without some adaptations.
Our children learn to do quite well
With visualizations.

Seeing how much time is left
Enhances their dimension.
When they can see the boundaries
There's much less apprehension.

Products on the market
Help the learner know
How much time already passed
And how much time to go.

Some may need an hourglass
To see the falling sand.
A buzzer, bell or wristwatch
Help others understand.

Another timer shows
A decreasing field of red.
Anxiety becomes reduced,
There's confidence instead.

Make telling time more tangible
So these folks comprehend.
They need to see time passing
From beginning to the end.

Essential Expert

For wisdom on the subject
Of environmental needs,
The occupational therapist
Is the one who intercedes.

He can find solutions for
Thumb sucking and biting.
He addresses eating needs
And strategies for writing,

Clothing adaptations,
Self-abuse inflictions,
Safety precautions
And working conditions,

Adapted home appliances,
And useful exercise,
Grasping and releasing
With ways to improvise,

Hygiene concerns,
Computer access,
Ideas for games,
And recreation success.

For persons on the spectrum
To reach their full potential,
The occupational therapist
Teaches skills that are essential.

Beyond Textbooks

Learning moments motivate,
They have significance,
When teachers share with openness
Their personal experience:

Problems she has conquered,
And finally worked through,
Lessons she has learned in life,
An experienced point of view.

When students know their teacher
Has been down that road before,
It sets the stage for learning
And strengthens her rapport.

Students need to have the skills
For choices they will make.
Experience is effective
If we learn from each mistake.

Learning from experience
Boosts appreciation;
It has a stronger impact
Than textbook information.

Give students learning moments
With a candid, open sharing.
Persons on the spectrum
Are inspired by such an airing.

Social Set-Ups

Teachers can bolster
Social success
With familiar routines
That student's address:

Let Jason practice
A suitable greeting,
Or participate in
His I.E.P. meeting.

Give Erin a job
When teaming with Heather,
To compete in a game
By working together.

Set-up a drama
To express courtesies,
Including the use of
"Thank you" and "Please."

Good teachers provide
A social skills stage
Where kids on the spectrum
Can learn to engage.

Taking Perspective

Before we engage
In shared conversation,
We try to fit in
To exchange information.

We listen to others
To share and express
And stay on the subject
So not to digress.

If the topic is sorrow
We offer support.
It's no time to give
A weather report.

When relatives visit
They need a reception.
It's the wrong time to show them
A CD collection.

In each conversation
We stay with the flow
To inform and enjoy,
To listen and know.

Be alert and observant
When taking perspective,
And stay on the subject
To be more effective.

Beginning Stages

A child develops reading skills
And fosters comprehension,
By starting out with picture books
With careful supervision.

The child begins to practice
Word articulation.
With help she makes predictions
From picture information.

As the child progresses
With guidance through some questions,
She's led to see relationships,
Concepts and connections.

She learns to form opinions;
The sequence of events.
With guidance she can also learn
To make an inference.

With story repetition
There's reading satisfaction.
These beginning stages
Make reading an attraction.

The goal is to facilitate
With pictures that she reads.
When words are paired with pictures
Her reading growth proceeds.

The Art of Disguise

When strategies are needed to boost
Communication,
Sometimes teachers improvise a scene where there's
Temptation:

Call on a student but use the wrong
Name.
Will he correct you and give you the
Blame?

Hold the booklet upside
Down.
Will he then tell you to turn it
Around?

Show him a snail but call it a
Snake.
Will he let you know that you've made a
Mistake?

Leave out a word in a rhyme or a
Song
To tempt him to speak up and tell you you're
Wrong.

Point to your nose but call it a
Cheek,
An enticement to get the student to
Speak.

Leave the price tag attached to your
Hat.
Will he allow you to get away with
That?

Engage in a game with his turn
Deleted.
Will he then complain, "I've just been
Cheated."

Some teachers use the art of
Disguise
To tempt their students to
Vocalize.

Communicative Intent

Take note when there's a tantrum,
When children disobey.
Analyze the circumstance,
And what their actions say.

What is the antecedent
That caused the altercation?
The goal is then to modify
Or change the situation.

Make sure they're not rewarded
If they have not complied.
They'll take what they can get
Each time you let them slide.

They need to see advantages
For showing good behavior,
That doing what's expected
Is always in their favor.

When children have a tantrum
Or express their discontent,
What do they communicate?
What is their intent?

The Meltdown

A meltdown is not the time to reason or
Correct,
Wait till she is in control to think and to
Connect.

Because of her anxiety and sensory
Commotion,
Productive interaction is distorted by
Emotion,

If other folks are present, they increase the
Tension.
They only add anxiety and amplify
Dissension.

Make sure your words and actions signify
Concern.
When the time is right, help the child to
Learn.

There seldom is a one-time fix, yet through
Education,
Teachers make a difference through skillful
Motivation.

The Token Transaction

Some teachers use a system
Where tokens are received.
The student gets rewarded
When behaviors are achieved.

Rules become established.
Tokens are recorded.
When he has earned the right amount,
The child is then rewarded.

He may earn a tangible,
Computer time or food;
It may be a social gift
Or quiet interlude.

The goal is for the student's
Behavioral success,
To learn to make good choices
By his own thoughtfulness.

Students on the spectrum
Need such regulation.
Visuals will also help
For self-evaluation.

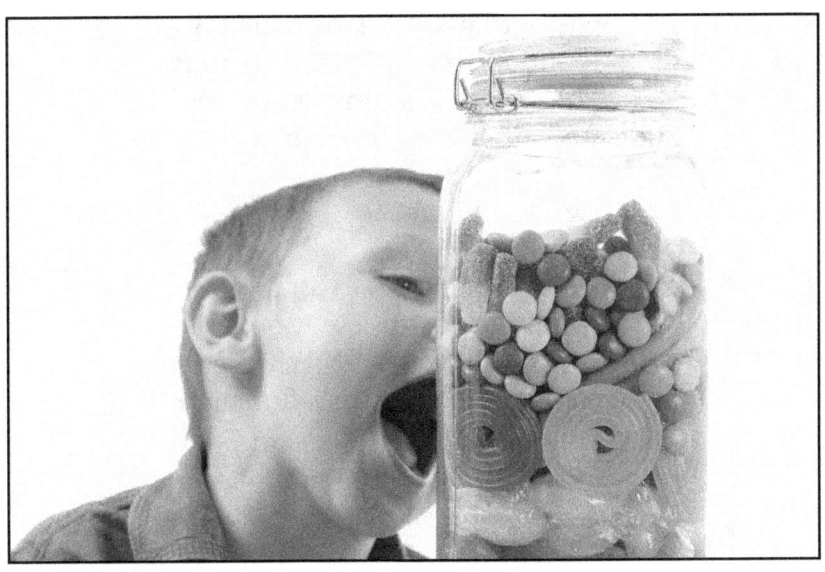

The Etiquette Factor

Appropriate behavior
Always makes a difference.
When people see we're out of touch
They tend to make an inference:

Habits outdated – Image deflated,
Clothes out of style – Diminished profile,
Low inhibition – Creates a suspicion,
Rude and intrusive – Makes folks elusive.

Yet

Well groomed and dressed – Favorably impressed,
Age-appropriate taste – Easily embraced,
Controlled and collected – Nicely accepted,
Apt conversation – Earns affirmation.

For people on the spectrum
Good manners are essential.
Etiquette instruction
Improves these folk's potential.

Between the Lines

Many people need some time
To think about a question,
In order to respond at will –
Not forced or by suggestion.

They may have to readjust,
To think and then react.
For the person with autism
Sometimes that's a fact.

It takes time to process
A multi-task request.
Language needs decoding.
There's much to be addressed.

Teachers must distinguish:
Is he cooperating?
Is he in need of guidance
Or just procrastinating?

Teachers read between the lines.
To search for information.
They deal with problems on the spot.
There's always fluctuation.

With pride they're innovators.
Few people are like these.
They're problem-solving specialists.
They have the expertise.

Let It Go

When thoughts from the past harass and
Attack
Let go of the worries and don't look
Back.

Positive health, friends and
Relations
Are far more essential than bad
Situations.

Kindness, mementos and lessons you
Hold
Are even more precious than silver and
Gold.

Expect to continue with good times and
Friends,
With promises, thoughts and work that
Transcends.

Let good thoughts abound since life goes by
Fast.
You'll find there's no future when you live in the
Past.

Choices

For children on the spectrum
Choices are restricted.
Without such independence
Despair can be predicted.

For happiness and self-esteem
Choices are essential.
Indeed the chosen outcome
Is always consequential.

For self-determination
They need autonomy.
Choices bolster confidence
As well as dignity.

Teachers are aware of this
So they have strategies
To give their students choices
And inform their families.

Choices bolster social skills,
With increased interaction.
When children feel included,
They have more satisfaction.

Give choices that are positive.
Use them as a lesson.
Acknowledge proper choosing
To encourage their progression.

Self-Reliance

Enterprising people
Are often quite well known
To be resourceful workers
As a team, or on their own.

They're sometimes called inventors.
They use imagination.
They're self-inspired to get it done
With sheer determination.

Autism spectrum children
Sometimes need instruction
At working independently
To strengthen their production.

Does he wait for the teacher
When he could ask a neighbor?
Some students need instruction
In resourcefulness behavior.

Demonstrate some study skills
That lead to independence.
Give these children strategies
To further their transcendence.

What are others doing?
Students need examples.
Teach them self-reliant skills
By showing them some samples.

Recourse Options

These children need a recourse,
A process that's in place
To vent their angry feelings
And talk about their case.

Give them some alternatives
For conflict resolution.
Let them know ahead of time
You'll help with their solution.

Make this process evident
To multiply their chances.
When they are given choices
Their self-control advances.

Once this view is understood
This process tends to boost
Cooperative behaviors,
And disruptions are reduced.

This procedure takes some time,
It's not done overnight.
Encouragement and confidence
Will help them get it right.

Predicting Sessions

We learn to make predictions
By reading people's faces.
We study body language
To enhance our social graces.

Children on the spectrum
Need such an education,
To make the right predictions
And use interpretation.

Show them with the sound turned off,
A TV presentation,
Or portions of a movie
To give their explanation.

Start guessing what will happen next.
What does that frown imply?
Did they see a happy face
And guess the reason why?

Through practice they can recognize
Gestures and expressions.
Our goal is to increase their skills
Through these predicting sessions.

Wrong Again

Don't think he isn't listening.
Don't think he can't perceive.
Don't think he's in another world
And therefore, can't receive.

Include him in your dialog
When he is with you there.
Make certain you're connecting
To show him that you care.

He may have a deficit
In sharing or expressing.
He may seem oblivious
Or even convalescing.

Still he needs acknowledgement
To know that he's accepted.
Everyone has feelings,
And they know when they're rejected.

Think he doesn't understand –
He doesn't quite fit in?
Think it doesn't matter?
You're simply wrong again.

Clutter

Children on the spectrum
Need visual organization.
Clutter is distracting,
It disrupts their concentration.

Do students see a tidy room
Where they can learn and play?
Are desks and tables clutter-free
Or is there disarray?

Reduce distractions where you can
To help with concentration.
Set a good example
To enhance their education.

They can keep their own desks clean
With training you provide.
It helps them be responsible
And they develop pride.

Neighborhood Bully

For lack of social understanding
Careless kids
Can be demanding.

It's often done
In ignorance,
An absence of self-confidence.

When teaching kids
With special needs
Stay vigilant of unkind deeds.

The teacher's job
Is to protect
From callous words and disrespect.

Students need
An education
For dealing with intimidation.

Folks can sometimes
Be unruly.
So watch out for the neighborhood bully.

Display of Confidence

Wall displays contribute to
Effective education,
But not when they're distracting
With too much stimulation.

Children with autism
Or Aspergers will need
Familiar words and pictures
That they comprehend or read:

Photos of the students,
The daily class routine,
Visuals of the classroom rules,
The morning circle scene,

Vocabulary pictures
And each child's work of art,
Familiar school activities,
The classroom seating chart.

Such established wall displays
Help students to address
A plan that helps them focus
To further their success.

Changing the Rules

We change the games that children play
So they can have success.
Achievement brings fulfillment
And takes away the stress.

A lower hoop for basketball
Gives children more control.
They play with more incentive
When they can make a goal.

A ball that moves much slower
Enhances confidence.
It's more relaxed and safer
When there is less suspense.

A safety seat for swinging
Increases relaxation
And makes it easy for the child,
To play with less frustration.

A batting tee for softball
Will help the child progress.
Change the games that children play
So they can have success.

The Trailer Outback

In some schools you'll still find
Programs not designed
For kids with disabilities.

These schools may win some honors
But there's one thing they still lack.
The kids with special needs
Are in the trailer parked outback.

It's a stigma on society
That gives it notoriety,
A glaring blight that's still around today.

Are equal rights for certain ones
While others are rejected?
Are special education kids
Simply not accepted?

We progress as a nation
Through inclusive education.
It's tolerance that leads us to achieve.

This concept, Helen Keller said,
Is learned in education.
Wherever there's intolerance
We find discrimination.

Words are just a clanging gong
When deeds are proven wrong.
Actions send a message that's quite clear.

We need to fix the problem
When we clearly see there's slack.
That trailer sends a message,
The one that's parked outback.

He's the Man

Ryan is quite talented
When he's telling jokes.
His brand of stand-up comedy
Connects with many folks.

Although he's on the spectrum
You would never know it.
When he's doing comedy
His manner doesn't show it.

Riddles, jokes and jargon
Are how he draws attention.
But some jokes we must censor.
They're too uncouth to mention.

He entertains you on the spot
By pointing out a gaffe.
He remembers punch lines well
And gets a hearty laugh.

Humor is a useful way
To strike up conversations.
For some folks on the spectrum,
It sets up good relations.

Here's a way to lighten up.
Promote it when you can.
When it comes to humor,
Ryan is the man.

Flexible Thinking

Leah tends to be rigid in her thinking
So the teacher helps her visualize
Different ways to organize:

By association
Location
Length
Position
Alphabetical order
Height
Strength
Composition

She's learning that it's acceptable
To be flexible.

Hidden Pain

There may be hidden pain
When you hear your child complain,
But the reasons may be hidden from your view.
They're painful to the child,
So be alerted, here's a few:

Acid reflux, Constipation,
Gastro-intestinal inflammation,

A painful toothache, anxiety and fear,
A piercing sound in the ear,

Sinus, headache, fearful dreams,
Flickering fluorescent beams.

Be alerted to the signs
Since some kids can't explain,
Why they're in discomfort.
Be aware of hidden pain.

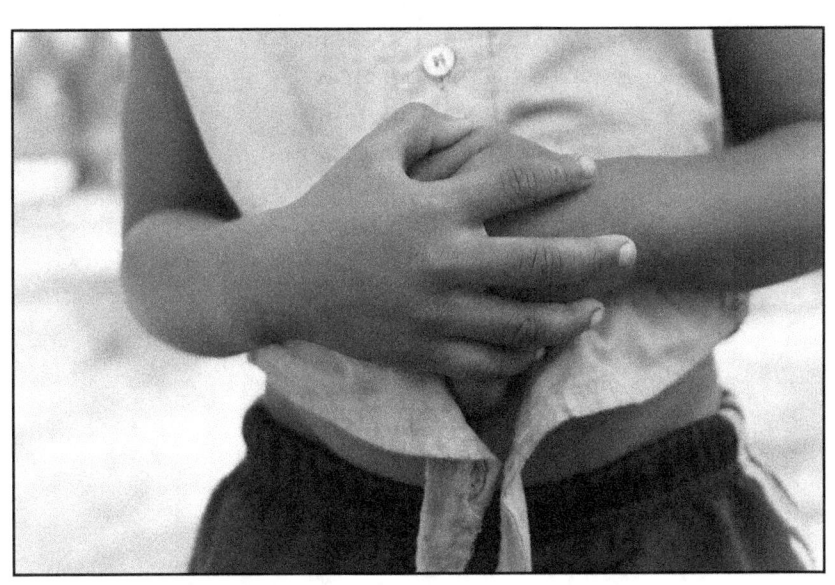

Exercise Issues

Some children on the spectrum
Lack motor skill control.
It may be hard to catch a ball
Or kick it to a goal.

They may lack agility
Or panic in a crowd.
Game participation
May simply be too loud.

They're known to have imbalance
With sensory connections,
Or trouble with perception
And following directions.

Yet when given motor skills
With careful adaptation,
They'll have reduced anxiety
And less perseveration.

The adaptive P.E. teacher
Is the expert to address
Game participation
And motor-skill success.

Need ideas for changing games?
Participation questions?
The adaptive P.E. teacher
Can give you some suggestions.

If

If socialization
Doesn't meet the expectation,
Find an accommodation.

If he's stressed
From over-stimulation,
Try relaxation.

If he has
Insufficient vocalization,
Try Facilitated Communication.

If a change
Meets with opposition,
Train him before the transition.

If it's a gastro-intestinal condition,
Seek the advice
Of a knowledgeable physician.

If a parent
Has resource questions,
Be prepared with your suggestions.

The Serotonin Factor

Does too much Serotonin
Cause over-stimulation
And impede concentration?
It's a cause for speculation.

This neurotransmitter
Affects our sleep and mood,
Perception, learning, memory,
Thoughts and attitude.

One group has higher levels –
The autism population.
Does this influence autism?
What's the implication?

People on the spectrum
Are prone to fluctuation.
There are so many factors
That control each situation.

Yet there's hope for breakthroughs
Where research is involved.
We're following this matter
Till these mysteries are resolved.

The Smokescreen

Todd seldom perceives
When someone grieves.

When a friend is dejected
It's not easily detected.

A display of comedy
Is often a mystery.

An expression of jubilation
Escapes his interpretation.

Fiction or non-fiction
Is a difficult prediction.

Since it's hard to relate
He simply doesn't participate.

Remove the body language disguise
By giving him ways to visualize –

A training routine
To overcome the smokescreen.

A Few Things to Try

A demonstration for clarification,

Compliments to motivate excellence,

Recreation to replace self-stimulation,

Deep breathing to counter the seething,

A visualization to bolster interpretation,

Velcro will do until she can tie her shoe,

Game adaptation to eliminate frustration,

A quiet zone when she needs to be alone,

Facial interpretations to enhance relations,

A weighted vest so she doesn't get stressed,

A one-step direction until she makes the connection.

Anxiety Exposure

We've learned from Donna Williams
Through her expert consultation
That anxiety exposure
Has a serious implication.

When persons on the spectrum
Feel their world has been invaded,
They may change the subject
A sign they're irritated.

Some refuse to interact
In the presence of a mate.
Avoidance and destruction
Are signs they can't relate.

Seething rage and anxiousness
May thwart a celebration,
When Tara lacks the social skills
To join the conversation.

Some people may retaliate
For lack of a connection.
All of these responses
Are a means of self-protection.

There are things that we should know
As Donna has suggested.
Excessive, constant praise
Is sometimes not accepted.

Use indirect approaches
That are brief and non-demanding,
With concepts that are simple
To bolster understanding.

Try role play with a puppet
To take away the stress.
These are some approaches
That may give the child success.

SECTION 2

Comments from parents and relatives

Partnership

I like my daughter's teacher, in whom I do confide.
She partners with each parent and gives her students pride.

Her successful outcomes are wonderfully inherent –
She treats the students with respect
And works with every parent.

She addresses students' needs and gives them self-esteem.
Good things tend to happen by working as a team.

Her expertise is clearly seen in children with autism.
She often gives me strategies as well as optimism.

Parent Priorities

Whether daughter or son
You know your child better than anyone.

So defend the things that your child needs.
Be organized so he succeeds.

Keep good records like a clerk.
Record the methods you've seen work.

Chart your loved one's education
And behavior information.

Keep track of health and vaccinations,
Food concerns and medications.

This is useful information
For research study participation.

With classroom staff cooperate.
Be your child's voice and advocate.

Equip yourself with useful tips
To guide your child's relationships.

Through it all, the parent learns
These consequential main concerns.

Gross Incompetence

My three year old has Aspergers
With outbursts quite overt.
I needed expert counseling
Before someone got hurt.

A pediatric doctor
Gave his point of view.
That's when I came to realize
This doctor had no clue.

I explained the tantrums,
The screaming and fixation.
His advice I clearly saw
Was only speculation.

"Your child will soon outgrow this stage,"
He said with some pretense.
That's when I saw how glaring was
His gross incompetence.

That experience taught me well,
It pays to shop around.
Next time I'll go elsewhere;
I need advice that's sound.

The Optimist

My child learns with picture cards,
They help her to express.
Such communication
Takes away some stress.

Picture cards at home and school,
That's how she organizes.
She needs to know what's happening
So there are no surprises.

Routines are a way of life,
We've learned to live that way.
Any sudden change of plans
Can wreck a perfect day.

She likes to move her picture cards
When each task is completed.
Throughout the day she gets rewards,
To show that she succeeded.

She needs to be encouraged.
Sometimes she needs defending.
I'm often teaching social skills.
My job is never ending.

I'm parent, teacher, advocate.
I keep my optimism.
I dare not get discouraged
'Cause my child has autism.

On a Mission

I'm fond of my support group.
Each month we get together.
It helps to know I'm not alone
For struggles that I weather.

Experts team with parents.
We're learning how to cope.
Loved ones need our vigilance
But parents sure need hope.

People on the spectrum
Need answers that we're after.
We get our strokes from experts
And share some fun and laughter.

"I need the right physician,"
Explained an anguished mother.
By sharing our experiences
We learn from one another.

Needs may run the gamut:
Behavior, social skills,
Medication, allergies,
Or how to pay the bills.

We can struggle on our own
But I've come to discover,
There's strength in numbers on this road;
That's why we need each other.

I realize the help I need
Means staying in the loop.
We're parents on a mission;
Support is in this group.

The Mystery

An autism cure is our aim.
Our children we want to reclaim.
Diverse is each history.
The cause is a mystery.
All differ, none are the same.

Some answers from research we've gained.
Teachers are now better trained.
Our battles we choose.
We win and we lose.
Our own health we must maintain.

Some new skills my son needs to learn.
Priorities I must discern.
I've made some mistakes
But I'll do what it takes
Because he's my major concern.

The Road Ahead

I need to teach my son quite well
For someday I'll be gone.
He needs to learn so many skills
So he can carry on.

Will the world be kind to him
Or will he be mistreated?
Will I live to see the day
Autism is defeated?

Will he have some solid friends
With whom he'll be connected?
Will he have the social skills
To always be protected?

He'll need supported living
And daily vigilance.
May kindness be his lot in life
Whatever his existence.

We're training for the road ahead.
It's tough but I'll be candid.
I'm giving him the tools he needs
So my son won't be stranded.

The Savant

She remembers things quite well
Like dates and names and faces.
Her photographic memory puts things in all their places.

When she hears an unknown song,
There's no need to rehearse.
She plays it on the keyboard both forward and reverse.

She's self-taught on the keyboard – no music education.
Her auditory memory defies an explanation.

"My memory," she says, "is like a digital recorder.
When I do the replay I visualize the order."

Skillful with a paint brush, she has artistic vision.
She can reproduce a scene with beauty and precision.

Yet this savant has gone through life
In fear and constant stress,
Since she was born without a means of social skill finesse.

Who can stomach such a life of anguish and chagrin,
To face another anxious day and know you don't fit in?

She once attempted suicide to get beyond the fray.
A friend came to her rescue, or she'd be dead today.

Changed Forever

Like every parent out there
I want the best prognosis.
My son is on the spectrum with
Asperger's diagnosis.

I want for him acceptance
Throughout society,
For him to be included
And be all he can be.

I must make prudent choices
Of services he'll need.
I'll also need some training
To manage and succeed.

My husband and my children
Must join in this endeavor.
We have found that Aspergers
Has changed our lives forever.

Some families have been overwhelmed,
Their hopes and dreams divested.
When facing all these challenges,
Marriages are tested.

We'll need help from the experts.
Each sibling must be trained.
To find fulfillment in this life
Support must be maintained.

The journey lasts a lifetime.
We're tested heart and soul.
Through the struggles will we grow
Or will we lose control?

Known to Kill

Our six year old has allergies
With nagging stomach pain.
Lactose is the reason
Yet this she can't explain.

Non-verbal kids depend on us –
Take heed, evaluate.
Does the irritation come
From something that they ate?

Painful food intolerance
Makes our child aggressive.
But is the reason understood?
Have people been perceptive?

She falls backward on the bed,
This gives her some relief.
Some people are bewildered.
They stare in disbelief.

Could this be a tantrum,
This troubling distraction,
Or is it really stomach pain –
An allergy reaction?

By working with an expert
The lactose was removed,
The remedy discovered,
Her comfort then improved.

Teachers now are being trained
To make the right prediction.
They've come to know food allergies
Can cause severe affliction.

Gluten is another source
That makes her irritated.
Her diet now is gluten-free,
The pain eliminated.

Food allergies are known to kill,
They thwart metabolism.
The group that's most susceptible
Are persons with autism.

Parents and professionals
Have learned to be discreet.
For people on the spectrum,
Chart well the foods they eat.

Massive Orchestration

Matt repeats what others say,
A flaw in his expression.
He now receives speech therapy
To counteract regression.

Communicating orally
Requires sophistication.
Social, motor, sensory –
There's massive orchestration.

Many on the spectrum
Can't handle multi-tasking.
Since Matt has echolalia
He'll echo what you're asking.

Society has speaking rules,
Respond when it's your turn.
This is one of many rules
That plague him with concern.

He contemplates his circumstance –
The pressure and demand.
He doesn't see relief, but hopes
That people understand.

You're the One

We owe the highest accolades
To the heroes of our cause.
Your efforts for our children
Bring a fond round of
Applause.

As we navigate the mountains
And work around the boulders,
We have come to realize
We're riding on your
Shoulders.

For helping find the experts,
Concerns in education,
Agencies to serve our kids,
Support group
Information,

Your advice and dialog
Are valued beyond measure.
The strategies and tools you've shared
Have always been a
Treasure.

For persons on the spectrum
We acknowledge what you've done.
You are among the heroes.
We all know
You're the one.

Facilitated Communication

We thought she had no aptitude
For logic and cognition.
Our daughter has Aspergers
But hope was our position.

Severe perseveration,
And verbal limitation,
Our goal was to facilitate
Our child's communication.

I heard about a strategy
Where I would give assistance.
With resistance to her typing arm
We hoped to see a difference.

While I support her typing arm
My daughter types each letter.
It took a while to see results,
With practice she got better.

Now she is a grown adult
And doesn't need my presence.
We reached the goal we had in mind –
She types with independence.

Honored for her expertise,
Admired throughout the nation,
She helps us understand her world
Through her communication.

An author and a poet,
A keynote conference speaker,
She gives us insight to her world.
Researchers often seek her.

Still she has anxiety
And social escapades,
Yet she earned so many
Noteworthy accolades.

With logic and cognition
Beyond our expectation,
The strategy that worked for her –
Facilitated Communication.

Below the Surface

Some early childhood milestones were late in being met,
Now my son at age 14 struggles with these yet.

Some social and expressive delays are still remaining.
We're teaming with his teacher to reinforce his training.

He can ride a two-wheeled bike almost anywhere,
But unlike other children, his interest isn't there.

Test taking scores are often low; he needs accommodations.
It's simply hard to regulate his strong perseverations.

His living skill performance is discerned through observation.
An education plan is formed with all this information.

To score my son objectively, with candor and with purpose,
It takes more than formal tests to get below the surface.

Through It All

Each day when my son goes to school
I finally get relief.
It's peace and quiet for a while
Although the time is brief.

To find someone to babysit
Becomes quite problematic.
Not everyone can handle
Behaviors so erratic.

News media are making
The public more aware
Of persons on the spectrum,
Their behavior, needs and care.

Some police are being trained
To cope with folks like these.
There is a need to understand,
Avoiding tragedies.

Medical professionals
With special needs experience,
Are always few and far between,
Yet, they're a treasured preference.

Some churches have experienced staff
For my son's education,
So children on the spectrum
Can have participation.

I'm learning all the agencies
And experts to pursue,
To bypass all the pitfalls
And hoops that I've been through.

It's been tough but through it all
I've found a cause that's greater.
I've become an expert
Parent educator.

The Steel Deal

Diagnosed with Aspergers,
Our son needs close attention.
We know he has a better chance
With early intervention.

We got the news when he was three –
It came as no surprise.
Since birth we saw the signals
Before our very eyes.

Crying uncontrollably,
His tantrums were intense.
Strained were all relationships;
His world did not make sense.

Story books were torn apart,
The norm could not resume.
Household items broken,
We child-proofed every room.

Some friends became more distant.
They couldn't comprehend.
Others drew much closer.
We've treasured every friend.

No longer is our lifestyle
A burden or appalling.
We know the world we're living in
Is where we have a calling.

We didn't know it at the time,
But sometimes life empowers.
We pride ourselves in helping folks
With problems just like ours.

When going through the fires of life,
I've learned that steel will melt.
We have a choice to do the best
With cards that we've been dealt.

A Tedious Affair

I took her shopping at the mall
Where she was quite engaged.
Our window shopping went quite well
Till she became enraged.

She recalled an incident
That happened yesterday.
It wasn't settled in her mind.
This prompted her display.

A screaming tantrum she began
As shoppers were astounded.
Unaware of autism,
Concerned and yet confounded.

I tried to move her from the scene;
Her screaming quite profuse.
Some teenage boys were passing by;
They heckled, "Child abuse."

At long last we departed
This tedious affair.
That's when I educated
The strangers standing there.

I gave them each a card to read
About this mannerism.
And now a few more people know
The symptoms of autism.

The Testing Tactic

Children test adults quite well
To get the things they want.
They'll bend the rules so you must be
Absolutely blunt.

Young folks on the spectrum
Learn this trick quite well.
Some are masters of the art,
So parents must excel.

Make solid rules and hold your ground.
Don't give in or waver.
Reinforce the positive
And not the wrong behavior.

You'll pay a price for giving in;
Kids worsen if they're pampered.
The tumult then intensifies.
Their growth is only hampered.

Get expert help if needed
But find ways to connect.
Nurture with consistence,
Fairness and respect.

The Journey

Our son often demonstrates
A fussy appetite.
He seldom gets the rest he needs
When he's in bed at night.

He rocks his upper torso,
Even when he's seated.
His teacher gives him extra time
To get his tasks completed.

His heels will seldom touch the floor
When he's engaged in walking.
He hasn't learned to wait his turn
No matter who is talking.

He flaps his hands beside his face,
A need for stimulation.
Doctor Schmidt is helping us
Through his examination.

Since working with our doctor
We've made this observation:
Our son finally sleeps at night
Thanks to medication.

The journey he is facing
Is like a mountain climb.
I'm charting my son's progress
One step at a time.

Spinning Wheels

We gave our son a tricycle
Several months ago.
We hoped that he would ride it
But no interest did he show.

We thought he'd learn some motor skills
And use it as designed.
But his idea was not exactly
What we had in mind.

Indeed, he likes his brand new trike,
He found it has appeal.
He likes to turn it upside-down,
Lean close and spin each wheel.

The rushing wind against his skin
Provides a new sensation.
But his behavior clearly shows
He needs the stimulation.

He likes to watch the spinning wheels
And hear the clicking sound.
He holds a stick that strikes the spokes
Each time they spin around.

As parents we have learned to deal
With non-cooperation.
And yet we recognize his need
For sensory stimulation.

Bending the Rules

When my daughter speaks to me
She seeks to be accepted.
She needs to know with certainty
That she is not rejected.

She has a frequent ritual
That gives her affirmation.
When she's finished speaking,
We touch for validation.

To process verbal language,
Requires sophistication.
By touching hands, she has no doubt,
She knows there's confirmation.

It's strenuous to go through life
When there's no resolution.
However, this survival skill
Provides a safe solution.

She finds the rules so cumbersome,
That govern conversation.
I'll gladly bend the rules for her
So she'll have less frustration.

There is no price I wouldn't pay
To have her world make sense.
This is how we both connect.
To give her confidence.

Moving On

Our daughter has a full-time aide
At school where she attends.
The aide makes learning possible
And they've become good friends.

Learning is attainable
With this accommodation.
Without such help, my daughter
Could not access education.

She has been non-verbal
But types with diligence,
With the aide beside her
Providing confidence.

Included in an English class,
Each day the aide instills,
Behaviors that are fitting
And proper writing skills.

Through the years we've come to see
How much our child has grown.
But now she needs to move along
And make it on her own.

It's difficult to part with friends
Who've helped her with compliance,
But now she's at another stage,
It's time for self-reliance.

If You Please

I use to ask the question,
"Wouldn't it be nice
To live with some tranquility
All void of sacrifice?"

But through all my experiences
And people that I've known,
I've learned it's through the struggles
That I've profoundly grown.

It's going through the hard times;
That progress is astounding.
Unraveling the obstacles
Have given me some grounding.

I'll take the road with challenges
For certain, if you please.
I've learned there's no fulfillment
On the road of perfect ease.

It's working through the problems
Though they be deep and wide,
That give sufficient reason
For a life that gives me pride.

It's been a life of struggle,
This road that's called autism.
But dealing with the challenges
Gives me optimism.

Volume Control

Quite often when he's speaking
Shane's voice is much too loud.
When he's talking to a friend
You'd think it was a crowd.

We're showing him examples
In different situations,
The proper volume needed
For pleasant conversations.

He needs to know that friendships
Result through interacting.
Without the proper volume
His words become distracting.

Many on the spectrum
Have this same concern.
It's crucial to his happiness.
This skill he needs to learn.

Collaboration with a Dog

A Labrador Retriever,
We gave to our son Mel.
Would it fill a social need?
Only time would tell.

The dog was trained to be a friend
And work where there's a need.
We believed that such a pet
Would help our son succeed.

They've become the best of friends
While working as a team.
Mel is now the one in charge
As he gains self-esteem.

The Labrador Retriever
Has truly changed our son.
Mel has learned to care for him
And both are having fun.

An increased sense of calmness
Our son now demonstrates.
He also speaks a few more words
When he communicates.

The partnership has bolstered
His pride and competence.
Collaboration with a dog
Helps his world make sense.

The Essentials

We need so many things in life
Like pure life-giving water,
Affection for a loved one,
Pride in son or daughter,

Fulfillment in the journey,
Safe participation,
Peace that yields contentment,
To know appreciation,

Happiness and self-esteem,
To know that people care,
Genuine relationships,
And hope that comes from prayer.

For people on the spectrum,
These things are so essential,
To meet their many challenges
And reach their full potential.

My son has these hopes and dreams
That he wants to refine.
I've come to learn his basic needs
Are just like yours and mine.

Generalization

Rules give him security,
They keep his thoughts connected.
When someone violates a rule
He makes sure they're corrected.

He recalls the details
From many years ago.
He helps us out when we forget
'Cause he will always know.

"Your seatbelt isn't fastened."
"You're not supposed to smoke."
He'll remind you firmly
Of any rule you broke.

Staying safe and healthy
Is what he learned in school.
He only wants to keep you safe
When you forget the rule.

"You forgot to wash your hands."
"Your hair is much too long."
In his way of thinking
There's only right or wrong.

We're teaching, rules are not the same
In every situation.
Step by step he's learning
Generalization.

Mum's the Word

While in a public setting
Engaged in conversation,
A dialog between two friends
Is private information.

We're judged by what we say and do.
Therefore, we take perspective.
To make the right impression
We must be quite selective.

Our son needs to be aware
Whenever there's a crowd,
When sharing keep things private,
And never speak too loud.

We're teaching him that others watch
Our actions and expressions,
So think about what others think
Because we leave impressions.

When we're out in public,
Our actions are a factor.
It's like being on a stage
And often we're the actor.

We're teaching him the way to speak
And not be overheard.
If he can't keep it private
He's learning mum's the word.

Lingering Anxiety

She often knows the answer
To the questions that she asks,
Yet people unaware don't see
The crisis that she masks.

Lingering anxiety
Portrays my child's psychosis.
So I support my daughter
Who has this diagnosis.

Sometimes she feels she's all alone
Lost in a foreign land.
She needs to know I'm there for her
And that I understand.

I'm there for reassurance,
To give her my concern.
Then with words of counsel
I try to help her learn.

But counseling is needed from
A trained psychologist.
So many on the spectrum
Like her are still at risk.

Teaching basic social skills
Addresses this discord,
But counseling that's needed,
Most parents can't afford.

Theatrics

We role play with our daughter
To teach her social skills.
So she can learn by doing
As we coach her through these drills.

Conflict resolution,
How to greet a friend,
When to speak with privacy
Or deciding when to spend,

Proper table manners,
How to wait your turn,
All of these and many more
Are skills that she must learn.

Role play can be stressful
When acting out frustrations
But it's private and supportive
In these learning situations.

She now asks to role play.
We're pleased that she's receptive.
She brings her problems to us
So we know it's been effective.

Backup Plans

Sometimes I need to find
Experienced respite care.
For children on the spectrum,
This service is quite rare.

It's even problematic
To get my child connected
With a child-care center
Where autism is accepted.

So I've become creative
To meet my child's demands.
Parents need alternatives
To carry out their plans.

Few will have the training
To deal with such behavior,
But there's a way that works for me,
I've trained my friend and neighbor.

The Quiet Zone

When dealing with anxiety
Juan needs self-stimulation.
He finds ways to ease the stress
Through sensory sensation:

He hums a sound in monotone
Or flaps his hands in silence.
These are ways he gets relief
For sensory imbalance.

When troubled with anxiety
Juan needs to be alone.
The place that he recovers best
Is called a quiet zone.

It's a place with no demands
All void of stress or fears.
We're teaching him some social skills
To practice with his peers.

We're working with his therapist
On ways to intervene:
A chewing tube, soft music,
And a mini trampoline.

Appropriate behavior is what we reinforce.
Step by step we're working on this goal.
We're thankful as the years go by
He's gaining more control.

It Comes Down to Respect

We all deserve autonomy,
Rights and dignity.
Self-esteem necessitates
Respect for privacy.

To barge into a bedroom,
Or any private space,
Infringes on one's dignity,
Which no one can embrace.

To violate a person's space
Intrudes upon his pride.
Don't expect such people
To welcome you in stride.

So with a knock upon the door
Request an invitation.
This habit also sets the tone
For good communication.

Parents, siblings, relatives
Must give this issue thought.
Don't assume it's understood,
This concept must be taught.

Everyone needs privacy.
It comes down to respect.
At home or in the business world,
That's what we all expect.

Finding Favor

Bolster your child's confidence –
Show him you're gratified.
Find ways to give him credit,
To build self-worth and pride.

Help him write or dictate
A good thing in his day.
Put it in a journal
To read or to display.

Start a two-way dialog
Between the home and teacher.
When there is something positive,
Both can stress that feature.

Teach through Social Stories,™
Behavior skills he needs.
Help him overcome mistakes
So he learns and succeeds.

Set the stage so he can be
Received as friend and neighbor.
Simply stated these kids need
Skills that garner favor.

Detour Ahead

Independent children
Are what this couple planned,
But when that didn't happen
Time helped them understand.

Their child had never reached the stage
Of self-sufficient living.
They realized that life goes on –
The world does not stop spinning.

They also made adjustments
As years had come and gone.
That unplanned road was difficult,
But still they moved along.

Like everyone, they journeyed
With hopeful dreams and plans.
They had come to realize
All things are in God's hands.

Sometimes a journey changes,
Like unexpected weather.
Still this couple learned some things
On this road together.

They met a detour in the road,
And yet their plans succeeded.
This journey that they chose to take
Was just the road they needed.

Detours on the road of life
Can lead to optimism.
They now write books that parents need
For dealing with autism.

The Thank You Issue

A gift received at holidays
Or any celebration,
Provides the opportunity
To show appreciation.

Make it fun and easy
For the child with special needs.
She can write or dictate,
But see that she succeeds.

The child can send a thank you note
Acknowledging the gift.
There's a lesson in this project
That gives the child a lift.

A natural environment
For social skills and writing,
Provides the child with competence
When the task is made inviting.

Perfection doesn't matter
But working as a team,
Builds a useful life skill
And bolsters self-esteem.

Food Disguise

Some children with autism
Have food sensitivities:

The crunch of a cracker
Sounds too piercing.

The texture of pudding
Feels too slimy.

The taste of an egg
Is too repulsive.

The feel of oatmeal
Has no appeal.

A hamburger and fries
Chopped in the blender
May look obscene,
But some children crave this routine.

Others will eat
One food item only.

Some children have developed
An unhealthy eating attitude,
Therefore, parents hide
Nutrition in their food.

They specialize
In food disguise.

What Are They Thinking

Indeed the high school drop-out rate
Alarms us in this nation.
Yet many students blossom
With a life skill or vocation:

Auto shop
Construction trades
Horticulture
Woodworking
Welding
A music skill
Cooking and
Homemaking

Many schools don't offer vocational education.
Can someone give me an explanation?

It's like going on a voyage
And yet the ship is sinking.
What are they thinking?

High Tech Tutor

It's a high tech invention,
That clearly adds spice –
A digital tablet,
The iPad® device.

Its portable size
Is a user convenience.
With numerous programs
To enhance independence.

It provides instant feedback
And high motivation
With visual features
And smart animation.

Students can learn
Through language arts drills,
Speaking instruction
And fine motor skills,

How to interpret
Facial expressions,
The feelings of others
And artistry lessons.

There's social skill training
And logic instruction.
Rewards can be earned
For successful production.

With this innovation
Many folks have progressed.
For the autism spectrum,
Countless needs are addressed.

SECTION 3

Comments from persons on the autism spectrum
and innovations by Temple Grandin and
Daniel Paul Tammet

Miss Perry

Miss Perry is my teacher, the kindest friend I've known.
When she sees I'm getting stressed, she has a quiet zone.

A place with things I like to do, a space where I can rest.
I just need some time away whenever I get stressed.

I make repeated vocal sounds; It's called perseveration.
It happens every time I get too much stimulation.

It frustrates me when I can't talk;
That's why I sometimes scream.
They're helping me find better ways to vent and let off steam.

If you suppress my screaming, I then become contrary.
The quite zone relieves the stress, that's why I like Miss Perry.

The Real World

My mother does the hard work,
She advocates for me.
That's why I'm now included
In regular P.E.

She knows I need some friendships
And school diversity.
Inclusion lets me learn from them
And they can learn from me.

I've often been excluded.
With insult I've been labeled.
Must I be segregated
Because I am disabled?

Must I do my banking at
A bank for the autistic?
I need accommodations
But let's be realistic.

Exclusion serves no purpose
When I need self-reliance.
Prepare me for the real world
And you'll get my compliance.

Drive-Throughs

I like fast food restaurants. To eat out is a treat.
I've memorized the menus at restaurants where I eat.

Sometimes I lose the privilege 'cause Mom says I must learn
That eating in a restaurant is a privilege I must earn.

Once I earned the privilege but tested mom's conviction.
I threw a tantrum on the floor. She put me on restriction.

From a public spectacle to the car with swiftness.
Forget the food and public scene,
'Cause my mom sure meant business.

From then on we did drive-throughs.
I learned by trial and error.
Mom orders from the window when I'm a holy terror.

"Can I eat in a restaurant?" Mom's response was, "Never,
Until your conduct proves to me
You've got your act together."

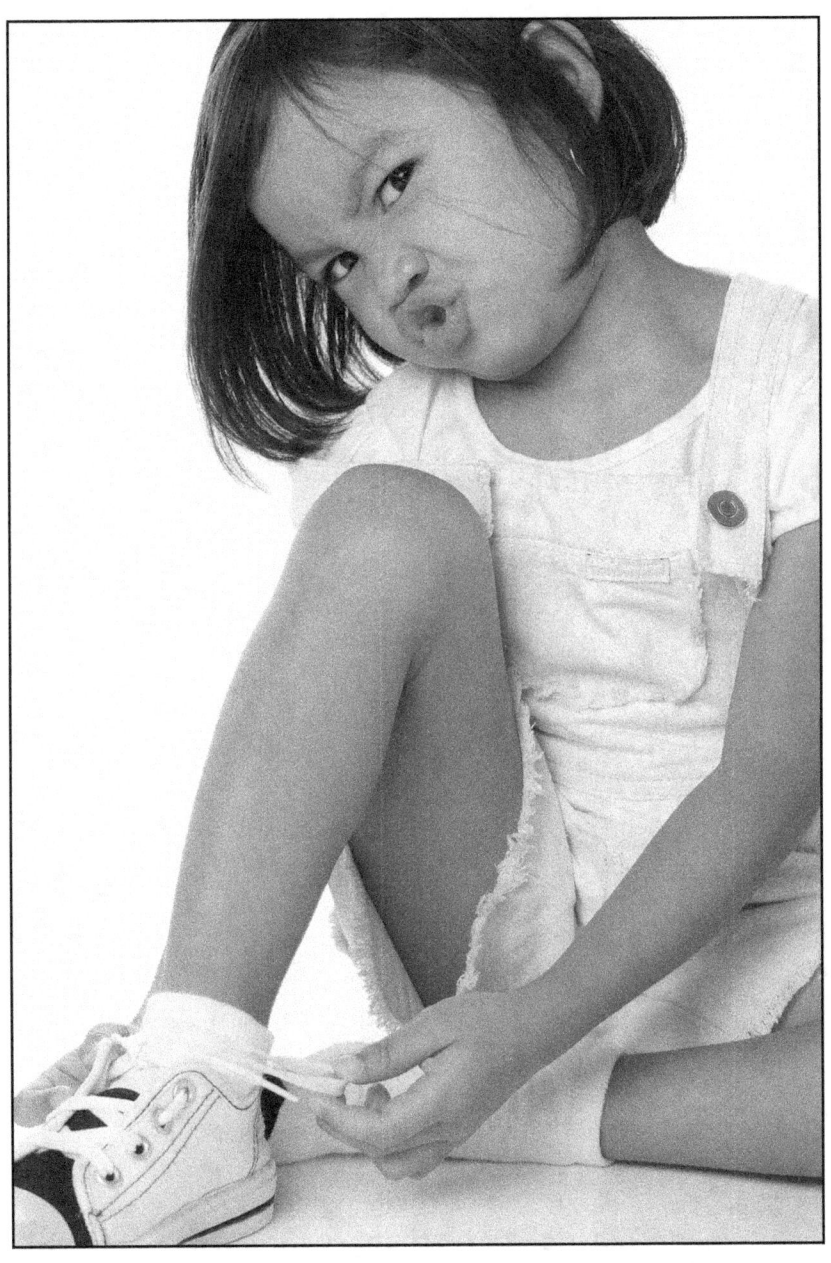

Undue Provocation

I've often been exploited
With undue provocation.
Indeed I've been the victim of
Overt discrimination.

Not so many years ago
We lived by unjust rules.
Disabled students were denied
Access to our schools.

Equal rights for everyone
Gives liberty its spark.
Exclusion of disabled folks –
Is where we missed the mark.

Through protest we've made progress
Reinforced by laws.
We've battled for our dignity
And broken down some walls.

There's now more public access
With each accommodation.
Laws now give us rights to learn
Through public education.

I'm thankful for those pioneers,
Champions of my cause.
I'm riding on their shoulders,
Those folks who changed the laws.

Confrontation

When I can't say the things I want
I'm trapped in my frustration.
These tearful moments propagate
My strong perseveration.

My mother seems to know my thoughts
And often speaks for me.
Her wish for me is more control
And less anxiety.

Sometimes people don't perceive,
These moments when I'm stressed.
And so I'm reprimanded,
My problem not addressed.

Words alone are hard to grasp
So show me as you speak.
Make use of all my senses,
That's the best technique.

Help me to express myself,
I need the confirmation.
Unless you find a way for me
There'll be a confrontation.

Terrifying Sounds

Loud noises always frighten me;
The clamor makes me frantic.
It's like I'm trapped with no escape.
Such terror makes me panic.

Mom's electric sweeper
Frightens me to tears.
She uses it when I'm not home.
It's too much for my ears.

I'm fearful of the noises
In a gambling casino –
Those ringing bells and mystic sounds
In Vegas or in Reno.

I use to run from piercing sounds,
But now I block each ear.
I detect so many sounds
That other folks don't hear.

I know I'm hypersensitive
But this I'd like to share.
I'm learning how to compensate
'Cause sometimes life's unfair.

Hidden Rules

I may not look you in the eyes
When we're in conversation.
I may even leave the room
In fear and trepidation.

The hidden rules in dialog
Make my struggle dire.
Unfamiliar people
Add fuel to the fire.

Idioms and similes
Keep me in suspense.
If I don't understand them
Don't laugh at my expense.

I don't know when to start and stop
Throughout the conversation.
I can't interpret gestures well
To meet your expectation.

My questions may embarrass you
With private information.
My impulsive laughter
May not fit the situation.

It's hard for me to concentrate
When I'm communicating.
This reduces me to tears
Because it's so frustrating.

When people come to visit
I choose to stay away.
It becomes so awkward when
I don't know what to say.

When we go to someone's house
I find a hidden space.
It may be in their backyard –
I feel so out of place.

These hidden rules are hard to learn –
For me, they may take years.
They add to my anxiety
And prompt some hidden fears.

My Individual Education Plan

I'm going to a meeting
To plan my education.
They want to hear my point of view
And every aspiration.

My teacher and some other staff
Will share with Mom and me
About my school performance
And my ability.

For one class I'm included
And I know that I'm respected.
The teacher always welcomes me.
It's nice to be accepted.

My interests and my school work
Are things that we'll address.
They're planning for my future
And friendships for success.

Mother and my teacher
Will help when it's my turn.
By sharing my opinion,
This team can help me learn.

It's more than just a meeting
To plan my education.
I can practice social skills
Through my participation.

Supposition

A comb is always in my hand
No matter where I go.
This habit rather calms my nerves
But it's bizarre I know.

I like to hear the clicking sound
When stroking every prong.
People often stare at me
Wondering what's wrong.

I look a little out of place,
That I will confess.
But smokers have their cigarettes
To help relieve their stress.

I'm not exactly in my youth
At thirty-seven years.
But my comb drowns out noises
And takes away some fears.

When people see this habit
And tension on my face,
They reduce my status
To an unkind, lower place.

Don't assume I'm ignorant
Based on supposition,
Until you know just what it's like
To be in my position.

When people treat me rudely
And think I'm unaware,
It's plain to see their disrespect.
They must think I don't care.

Intolerance is a hurdle.
Their actions clearly show
That they are simply out of touch,
Or fear what they don't know.

Overloaded

Scratchy sweaters bother me,
They always hurt my skin;
Just like I'm being punctured
With a needle or a pin.

I don't engage in shaking hands
Or even giving hugs.
Whenever people touch me
It feels like creeping bugs.

A haircut makes me anxious
Because it gives me pain.
With every clip I feel my nerves
Signaling my brain.

I know my skin is sensitive
But often I feel trapped.
I can't shut off these irritants;
I'm trying to adapt.

Sometimes a visual overload
Takes me by surprise.
I've found a way that works for me,
I just close my eyes.

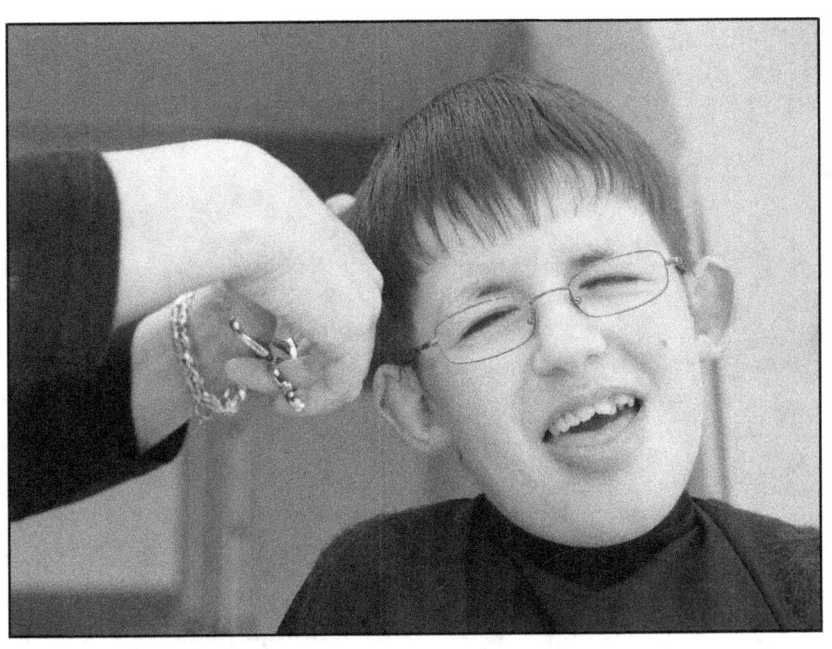

The Reality

I know that I'm a grown adult
But in reality,
I dream about my childhood,
And things I'd like to be.

I still like Disney characters,
Costumes at Halloween.
I always like to read about
A princess or a queen.

I like to feel the rushing wind
While riding in the car,
So I lean out the window
Though I know it looks bizarre.

I listen to the Beatles
And even sing along.
I know all their albums
And words to every song.

At malls I touch the mannequins
With curiosity.
I know they're only statues
But they seem real to me.

There's one thing that I'd like to have
Before time gets away.
I want to have a boyfriend
And marry him someday.

The Squeeze Machine™

Deep pressure to the body has been found to lower tension.
A Squeeze Machine™ has been designed
And used with that intention.

The inventor, Temple Grandin, through her investigation
Has found this method useful
For prompting relaxation.

Results from several studies have been tested and produced.
When the Squeeze Machine™ is used
Tension is reduced.

This discovery came about through cattle observation.
Deep pressure to their bodies
Produces relaxation.

Persons on the spectrum have been calmed by this solution.
Thanks to Temple Grandin for
Her useful contribution.

Diagnosed with autism, yet Temple's innovation
Transformed cattle handling.
She's the expert in our nation.

Idiosyncratic

Some of my behavior is
Eccentric, I'll agree.
I therefore, have a private life
The public doesn't see.

If people saw my other side
They'd find me problematic,
But I'll confess my comfort zone
Is idiosyncratic.

Behavioral disorder
Is the label people see,
But human condition
Describes it best for me.

Poles Apart

You can do more than one thing at a time:
Drink coffee and talk,
Gesture and walk,
Look me in the eyes
And listen at the same time.

Good friends but
Poles apart.

I see the bug on the leaf. You see the tree.
I hear the clock ticking,
You don't.
I see the mustache.
You see the face.

Good friends but
Poles apart.

Daniel Paul Tammet

Daniel has Aspergers,
Yet he's known for much success.
Numbers come with feelings;
He computes them with finesse.

Every date and number
Has its own identity.
With color, shape, size and form
And some endowed with beauty.

He also is a linguist,
An accomplished innovator.
He has an online service
As a language educator.

Daniel speaks Icelandic
Yet he studied just one week.
Many other languages
He also learned to speak.

He describes the way he thinks
To help us find solutions.
In research studies of the brain
He's making contributions.

An expert mathematician,
Some records he has set.
Need some inspiration?
Look up Daniel Paul Tammet.

Glossary

Accommodations: changes that allow for access or participation by an individual. Without these changes, the individual would be excluded from participation.

Adaptive Physical Education Teacher: a person who adapts sports and physical activities so persons with special needs can participate with more success than they would have in a regular physical education class.

Articulate: to express in a coherent verbal form.

Auditory Processing: the ability to interpret speech with sufficient speed and efficiency to comprehend spoken information.

Augmentative and Alternative Communication (AAC): communication devices or strategies for individuals with impairments in producing or comprehending written or spoken language.

Autism Spectrum (Autism Spectrum Disorder or the Spectrum): a pervasive developmental disorder characterized by a wide range or spectrum of conditions that present challenges in social interaction, sensory perception, motor skills and communication. There are five disabilities on the autism spectrum as defined in the fourth edition of the Diagnostic and Statistical Manual (DSM-IV):

1. **Autism:** a disorder with impairments in social interaction and communication as well as restricted

and repetitive patterns of behavior, interests and activities.

2. **Asperger's syndrome:** a diagnosis for persons with impairments in social interaction and restricted and repetitive patterns of behavior and interests. These persons have no clinically significant delay in language or cognitive development other than social interaction.

3. **Pervasive Developmental Disorder Not Otherwise Specified (PDDNOS):** a severe pervasive impairment in social interaction with impaired verbal or non-verbal communication skills, interests and activities. These individuals do not meet the definition for "autistic disorder" because of the late age at onset. They are too socially adept to be categorized as having autism.

4. **Rett's Disorder:** a genetic disorder that occurs almost exclusively in girls. Development is normal for the first six to eighteen months after birth. Then, there is a regression in systems influenced by the nervous system. Psychomotor, language, social and mental skills may be affected.

5. **Childhood Disintegrative Disorder:** these children develop normally the first few years of life. However, for unknown reasons, prior to the age of ten, there is a significant loss of previously learned skills in some or all of the following areas: communication, social interaction, bladder control, play or motor skills.

Chewing Tube: a toy designed to go into the mouth to provide sensory input and to develop motor skills required for speech, sound production, chewing and swallowing.

Communicative Intent: a non-verbal message that a person communicates by his actions.

Dyslexia: a learning disability characterized by difficulties in reading. Decoding and comprehension are notable challenges. This is not related to vision, hearing, or inadequate reading instruction.

Early Intervention: support services in education and health care for infants and young children who have developmental delays or are at risk of a disability.

Echolalia: involuntary repetition of words spoken by others.

Exposure Anxiety: the involuntary self-protective responses of avoidance, diversion and retaliation that occur when others or the outside world intrude.

Expressive Language: the ability to produce language in any of a number of modalities such as speaking, signing or writing.

Facilitated Communication (FC): a form of augmentative and alternative communication (AAC). A facilitator provides physical and emotional support to an individual who has difficulties with speech by pulling back on the typing arm to provide a constant resistance to the person who communicates by typing. Sometimes the person who is typing progresses to the point where physical contact by a facilitator is no longer needed as long as the facilitator is nearby.

Fine Motor: the use of small muscle groups necessary for such activities as writing, manipulation of an object and eye movements.

Generalization: the ability to apply a behavior or skill across different environments.

Gross Motor: the use of large muscle groups necessary for such activities as walking, running, sports and recreation.

Hidden Social Rules: rules that are usually not directly taught but are assumed to be understood. Social rules that most people perceive, "pick up," or learn from subtle cues or body language, are often not perceived by a person who has social challenges. Not knowing what the hidden rules are, will impact social interaction and a person's well being.

Hypersensitive: high and abnormal sensitivity to stimuli.

Inclusion: when persons with disabilities have access to or participation in activities with non-disabled peers for the purpose of learning or pursuing an array of skills not possible when they are excluded. Inclusion may occur with accommodations to enhance participation.

Kinesthetic: awareness of personal body position and movements.

Meltdown: when a person is overwhelmed with sensory overload. They may feel threatened or helpless. The resulting behaviors may include: hysteria, crying, exhaustion, sweating, steadfast refusal to cooperate, lashing out, hitting, biting, echolalic behavior, repetition of non-relevant phrases and stemming.

Motor Planning: the ability to plan and carry out a motor task, as well as make inferences about new ones, based on previous experience. The inability to motor plan can affect speech and language development and handwriting, as well as large muscle activities for sports and recreation.

Motor Skill: a learned sequence of movements that coordinate to carry out a motor task.

Neurotransmitter: a chemical in the nervous system that transmits nerve impulses in the brain.

Occupational Therapist: a person trained to help disabled individuals improve their ability to perform tasks in daily living and working environments.

Perseveration: the uncontrolled repetition of a behavior, word, phrase, gesture or motor action despite the absence of a stimulus. This usually occurs during stressful situations.

Pervasive Developmental Disorder: a group of conditions that involve delays in the development of many basic skills most often in communication, social and cognitive abilities.

Psychomotor: Mental events that result in motor outcomes or vice versa.

Receptive Language: language received and interpreted by the listener, reader or viewer.

Ritual: preoccupation with repetitive behaviors, movements or speech and rigid adherence to routines.

Savant: a person on the spectrum who is extraordinarily talented in one or more areas.

Sensory: reception of stimuli through the senses of smell, sight, hearing, touch and taste.

Sensory Overload: when too much information or stimulation is received at once. The inability to process or handle this information can result in a meltdown.

Serotonin: a neurotransmitter that regulates many functions including mood, appetite, learning and sensory perception.

Social Stories™: an instructional strategy developed by Carol Gray to provide information through a story to help a person handle a social situation appropriately. A teacher, parent or friend writes a story that addresses a social problem that a student is having. The teacher may tell the story from her perspective describing how she has successfully handled a similar situation. From introduction to conclusion, this non-threatening story provides information the student needs to be more effective when dealing with this problem in the future. Visuals may also be used for clarification.

Special Day Class: a classroom where special education students receive instruction for the majority of their school day.

Special Needs: persons who require special education services, supports or monitoring.

Squeeze Machine™: a device that provides deep pressure to the body to produce calmness. Temple Grandin, the inventor, observed that deep pressure applied to cattle in a cattle chute, had a calming effect. She then designed the Squeeze Machine™ that is now being used by some individuals with autism spectrum disorders.

Stemming (Self-stimulation): behavior such as hand flapping or rocking to stimulate one's own senses. This is often done to find equilibrium or to calm oneself.

Supported Living: services to support the needs of persons with disabilities. This may include such services as a personal assistant, house parents, mobility equipment, home adaptations, transportation or job supports.

Taking Perspective: the thought process that occurs when space is shared with another person. Persons on the spectrum sometimes have difficulty with the concept that we all impart impressions by the way we look, what we say and what we do. By taking perspective, we can monitor our behavior.

Transition: preparing a student for changes that occur in daily living. Transition steps are also involved when preparing a student for the changes that occur after high school graduation. Staff and family members assist the student in this process by identifying long-range goals, training and activities necessary to achieve these goals. This may include planning for vocational education, employment, adult services, independent living and community participation.

Visual Motor: the coordination of visual skills with motor skills.

References

Buie, T. (2007, February). *GI Issues in Autism*. Presented at the Anaheim Autism/Asperger's Conference, Anaheim, CA.

Falvey, M. (2005). *Believe in My Child with Special Needs!* Baltimore: Paul H. Brooks Publishing Co.

Ferguson, S. (Producer), Jackson, M. (Director). (2010). *Temple Grandin* [Motion Picture]. USA: HBO.

Freeman, B.J. (2009, April). *Update on Treatment for Autism Spectrum Disorders: What We Know*. Presented at the Greater Long Beach/San Gabriel Valley Chapter of the Autism Society of America, Long Beach, CA.

Grandin, T. (1995). *Thinking in Pictures and Other Reports from My Life with Autism*. New York: Vintage Books.

Gray, C. (2000). *The New Social Story Book*. Arlington, TX: Future Horizons.

Guber, P. (Producer), & Levinson, B. (Director). (1988). *Rain Man* [Motion Picture]. USA: MGM Studios.

Halvorsen, A.T. & Neary T. (2001). *Building Inclusive Schools, Tools and Strategies for Success*. Boston: Allyn & Bacon.

Irlen, H. (1991). *Reading By the Colors*. Garden City Park, NY: Avery Publishing Group.

Leaf, R. & McEachin, J. (Eds.). (1999). *A Work in Progress*. New York: DRL Books Inc.

Lautenschlager, J. (Producer), & Naess, P. (Director). (2005). *Mozart and the Whale* [Motion Picture]. USA: Millennium Films.

McGinnis, Ellen & Goldstein, Arnold P. (1997). *Skillstreaming the Adolescent*. Champaign, IL: Research Press.

McGinnis, Ellen & Goldstein, Arnold P. (1997). *Skillstreaming the Elementary School Child*. Champaign, IL: Research Press.

Myles, B.S., Adreon D. & Gitlitz, D. (2006). *Simple Strategies That Work!* Shawnee Mission, KS: Autism Asperger Publishing Co.

Myles, B.S., Trautman, M.L. & Schelvan R.L. (2004). *The Hidden Curriculum*. Shawnee Mission, KS: Autism Asperger Publishing Co.

Notbohm, E. & Zysk, V. (2010). *1001 Great Ideas for Teaching and Raising Children with Autism or Asperger's*. Arlington, TX: Future Horizons.

Shore, S. (2003). *Beyond the Wall*. Shawnee Mission, KS: Autism Asperger Publishing Co.

Tammet, D. (2006). *Born on a Blue Day*. New York: Free Press.

Westling, D.L. & Fox, L. (2004). *Teaching Students with Severe Disabilities*. Upper Saddle River, NJ: Pearson Merrill Prentice Hall.

Williams, D. (2004). *Not Just Anything*. London: Jessica Kingsley Publishers.

Wurzburg, G. (Producer/Director). (2004). *Autism Is a World* [documentary film]. Atlanta, GA: CNN and State of the Art, Inc. (Sue Rubin was the writer and subject of this Academy Award ® nominated documentary).

Index

www.ingramcontent.com/pod-product-compliance
Lightning Source LLC
Chambersburg PA
CBHW062148280526
45788CB00001B/347